THERE IS NO WAY TO CRACK THE EGG

THERE IS NO WAY TO CRACK THE EGG

THE FAILED SYSTEM OF LAW

HOW TO UNDERSTAND THE UNFAIR SYSTEM

DR. KEITH GAVIN
&
ANDREI SCHOLZ-JONES

To order additional copies of this book, contact:
Xlibris
844-714-8691
www.Xlibris.com
Orders@Xlibris.com
840961

CONTENTS

INTRODUCTION

A FTER A CRITICAL MOMENT of introspection and mental consideration concerning the state of the Afro-American community and the law, it has come to my attention that the law will never be fair to the so-called free black man and woman. The rules are built to keep the white majority in power. Unless there is a change in the constitution and the political structure of our nation, the laws must reach down to the very people who have been afflicted and abused by the direction of the Europeans and how they set it up.

The laws are not fair, the system is biased, and the constitution is based upon how they set it up to benefit from the privileges to pursue happiness and liberty—at the same time, leaving out the African American population, even adding in the 13, 14, and 15 amendments. Unless these three critical amendments are not changed and ratified, then the constitution will always fail the disenfranchised and poor in our community.

There must be a change in the legislation, and it must meet the critical needs of the people in every part of this American life we live. It will even help the law student better understand the law and the dynamics. The redistribution of wealth and fairness must be dealt with in the law and how people are treated in the court system. Bringing on a Black woman in the highest justice system may help the conditions, but she will have to fight and be stressed fighting the people to deal with their so-called social and political problems to reach a balance.

Hopefully, this book will provide you with some critical steps to ponder and share with like-minded individuals who understand the power of connection and mental revolution, critical thinkers, and individuals who truly understand the dynamics of this unfair system. They gave us their religion, and we used it to get ahead, but we have lost our way and need to go back to Kemet to understand how our ancestors are calling for us in America to confront the wrongs and take our place. Hotep

THE LACK OF SOCIAL AND POLITICAL POWER

B ECAUSE MANY AFRICAN AMERICAN was kept out of the economic process in America and were not given the same starting gate as others, they are playing catch up in a system that is bent on keeping them in the same place and spinning wheels to compete in the global community when it comes to social and political power.

The laws are not on their side, and those who can deal with the issues and problems in their districts are taught not to help their own. The real question that is looming for us to ponder is that African Americans have possessed the knowledge to control their social systems and political direction for centuries. What has happened is the Europeans came to Africa and saw what and how they moved socially, economically, and politically then stole what they needed and used it to help themselves understand the laws and collaborative process that governed the Africans.

This means that the Africans were too trusting and allowed them to trick them when they gave the Europeans their hand. They took the African school system of thinking and created a system of remembering instead of learning and developing their nation. Stealing is stealing regardless of how it is done. The mental review of the African is powerful and creative. There are tribal differences and cultural conditions that need to be worked out. With a steering committee or participatory action plan of cultural differences, Africans can deal with their own social and political problems.

If history has explained anything that the Africans have done politically is to teach the Europeans how to balance the checkbook and share resources. This is a known fact that Mansa Musa had social and political power during his reign that many Europeans could never fathom. His father was Faga Leye, son of Abu Bakr, one of the great thinkers and devoted religious individuals. Mansa Musa brought government bureaucrats and architects to help establish many state cities such as Mauritania, Senegal, Gambia, Guinea, Burkina Faso, Mali, Niger, Nigeria, and Chad.

The African Americans must understand that their laws came from the Africans in the motherland and have been changed from the proper knowledge. What has happened is that the social and political powers took the expertise and reconverted it into how they would rule others in and around them. This does not diminish the skills and abilities of the thinking of the African only shows you that the laws are derived from the knowledge of God's actual creation in our midst.

They helped the thinking and social construct of the political mindset of the Europeans. They have done to reconvert the review of the nations in a way that makes them seem to have done all this and excluded the mindset and power of the Africans. So how can we follow the laws against us as African Americans when the true nature of the law was maladjusted to keep many of us in bondage.

To gain the political advantage in our times, African Americans must begin to understand better the legal process and how it was developed and question the validity of the laws that govern if the rules were created. At the same time, enslaved people were still in the throes of American politics and the social norms debated among slaveholders in congress. Then how will and law be fair to those who were property during those times. There may have been some good-hearted Europeans not all of them were terrible people. But, like control and racial hatred, people can hide the truth in the law and still make it seem as they are with change but then reconvert that change.

Let's look at the laws then and know and compare the political landscape of justice in the court and how the laws benefit one group over another. Affirmative action was used to help lift impoverished communities out of the social underclass. But somehow, they used it to help European women come out and replace them with working women of color and underclass the African males in society. This, in return, opened the jail cells and educational construct to incarcerate many youths and unskilled in the community and lock them away.

The welfare system was created to depower the African black male from help in raising their offspring and give power to his woman rather than working out a family together. Therefore, emasculating him and bringing in a different man to assist her from the European perspective. This is not done by luck but by design. These were the same conditions that they have done to the mental structure of many African black males in the society where they believed that obtaining a European woman; they have secured the American dream and ladder only to find out that they are only used.

So, you go home to a secure structure with a constructed mindset that you have helped build the African American community by blending into the society under a false representation. The laws still apply that you are not part of the social structure regardless of who you commingle within the community to which you are born. The political perspective of how social and political power needs to be addressed is rewriting the law to fit a just society and balance the power.

The laws used in the United States legal system have been only used to govern social behavior and control the economic structure in the political and social construct. The rules keep the wheels moving toward individualism and not a collective process that helps the citizens on the shores of the United States.

Therefore, they created the 13th amendment before the 14th amendment, which says

… All persons **born or naturalized** in the United States and subject to the jurisdiction thereof **are citizens** of the United States and the State wherein they reside. No State shall make or enforce any law which shall abridge the privileges or **immunities** of citizens of the United States; nor shall any State deprive any person of life, liberty, or **property, without due process of law; nor deny to any person within its jurisdiction the equal protection of the laws…**

Immunities mean; officially granted exemption from legal proceedings.

Therefore, if the 13th amendment can take your liberties away by incarceration and keep you from being able to have life, freedom and you once were property, then we can be political by legal and social application keep you from the same rights and benefits by using the justice system to strip you of your born rights in a land that says it is governed by order and law.

Therefore, understanding the law and how it is governed will help any African law student better understand the dynamics of the law. What is the key to dealing with the law while studying the legal system in Europeans' minds? This is one of the reasons why it keeps failing us when we are fighting a mindset that is already used to keep us in check and balance.

Once you realize the game, you can better combat the courts' thinking and how they dispense justice when they see you, and then you can better understand why they allow the **African American black female** to make it through law school and only a few black men.

This is when the psychology and sociology of the process are developed, and it is not done by care but done to understand better the nature of the genius and charismatic knowledge of the African black male who has a Kemet connection. There are some factors that they use to gain that information. **Broken home, hatred of her father, a lack of financial stability in the community, or an African male to govern because of his lack of income.**

Once these models have been set into her mindset from the book they read and the process of the cases shown to them, it is easier for the system to figure out how to govern the so-called African black male. Remember the willie lynch process that they must trust in our system and depend on us; they must love and respect us only. If they cannot take care of their own needs and supply them, we will break their independence because of the capacity to take care of their offspring using the black female.

Therefore, the social and political structure of the legal system is created in this manner, which helps keep them in power because they have used this psychological process over the years to control the behavior of the masses. In law, Austin 1832, believed that we could keep the power if we look at the process and handle the individual's behavior. We are using legislative power through the courts and the law. This is one of the reasons we must better understand the social and political power of the legal system.

These are some of the critical factors why they do not want African black males to litigate in the court because they will better understand the nature of the beast. The educational articulation of critical thinking will become apparent. The rule of law will then be challenged because it does not include the African nature and regulations that govern the universe in which we live, where everyone is treated with due process and fairness in the legal system. This is another reason many African males are kept out of the jurisprudence course if you did not know it.

You must begin to ask yourself the questions, why? They set up the process in slavery to keep you from knowing how to read the books and bible to understand better the issues that govern your ability to be free thinkers.

Today, if they keep you out of the law schools and make it difficult for you to articulate the game, they can keep most communities in step with the law. Many African American lawyers are trying to figure out why they are losing the court cases because you do not fully understand the Latin meaning and how they fit into the circumstances.

Remember, they stole it from the **Africans, Greeks, Romans, Latins, English** from where they came and created the American legal system you know of today.

Therefore, by studying and developing a love for knowledge of self and social process and political moves of each group, your understanding of this failed system that seems unfair will come alive to you during your law years and economic performance of the social and political process.

UNDERSTANDING THE
LAW OF AMERICA

✻ THERE ARE THREE STRUCTURES to the laws we follow in the American justice system. **Common law, Roman law**, and **American law**. Let me explain the detriment or inculpate of the truth given in law. For me to exculpate for you the anecdotal process of law, you must understand the nature of the thinking of the Europeans and how it plays into the legal system.

Common law deals with how the Europeans brought the rules from England when they came to the United States. They left the same place and wanted to start a new and better way of thinking only to use as a base the same social, political, and legal system to govern the masses. That means they were still stuck on the same laws and power structures they came from and just added in some other social thinking to solidify how they would govern.

Roman law deals with keeping people in place by governing them in police states and regulations that help keep the people in power by forcing rules that keep the masses in lockstep to follow. Or they will put them in jail, sanction them and use the social and political power of dominance to control. This is how the system works to keep the same Europeans in control of their so-called system that they have created over time—saying in theory that it is changed from the English model that was only maladjusted to fit the same norms for society and political thought. They also gained Latin to insert it into the legal process to make you think they created the law.

American law deals with combining these legal theories and then creating a system that is unfair to the public and not representative to the citizens of the United States and the surrounding territories. The constitution that was developed did not include the enslaved people until the ratification of the so-called 13th amendment, which was a lie in the political sense and a social mess because of the thinking of Thomas Jefferson not only to keep a hand on the enslaved person but to use Roman law to enslave the same people it was so-called freeing.

They placed this in the constitution of the United States as a fake law.

Neither slavery nor **involuntary servitude, except as a punishment for the crime of which the party shall have been duly convicted**, shall exist within the United States or any place subject to their jurisdiction.

Suppose the enslaved person who was not given any rights before their rights were given according to the law be subjected to the people's rules in the constitution. What African American individual was there to consider this part of the law. African Americans still at the time were not fully represented by legal precedence in the court or the laws of the states.

This means that American law can and does what they always have done: create laws that help them keep who they want in involuntary servitude, making the masses believe that the law is fair. Therefore, unless this amendment is dealt with, the entire understanding of the law is a lie. Consequently, it will be hard to crack the egg, and the legal system will continually fail the African Americans, also the disenfranchised in our country.

By truly understanding the legal system's social and political makeup, the laws will be one-sided and marginalized to keep one group in power over the other groups if they do not follow the model set in place. When DNA came out, it started to call lies to account and confessions to crimes.

This thing DNA was already in Kemet 2000 years ago, in the tombs of the workers and the kings in the valley. It told the story of the people and the generations to check the truth out by following the trail. The Europeans stole it from them and made you believe they created the science.

When our ancestors speak, we listen to their spirits and trust that they lead us down the right path. The universe will align and help us if we trust the God, we know has always been there for us. How do we begin to crack the egg of the legal system and understand how to deal with the problems in the justice system? It is up to us who love right over wrong and will follow the path leading to the great IAM.

The American legal system was only developed from flawed men and women who came to get from under the rule of a king but made a law that seems to be governed under the same confusion and mess they came from to keep the power. If African Americans want to fix the problem, then the legal and justice system will have to be ratified and changed to fit all citizens into the equation. The **morals and integrity** of the justice system and the police departments must be reformed better to understand the pulse of each community and state.

The **biopsychosocial and economic conditions** must be dealt with if there will be any change to the political and social construct of the justice system. If any imposed criminogenic needs are to be met, they must come from the legal side of the justice system and legislative process. If the rule of America's justice system is to succeed, then a consorted effort must be made through leadership in the communities from groups, churches, synagogues, temples, and mosques. These critical committees must be established to change the social issues that lead to the power structure and the political means the legal system draws to enact change in the society.

Gomillion v. Lightfoot during 1960 shows us that dividing the electorate and making up the line to win districts is a process developed by the people who hold power. The issues we find in this example tell us that their reasons for law are deformed and need change to make sure it is fair and people have the right to decide fairly during elections.

The laws in America have good and bad decisions that have been decided on over its life structure. For the law student, the African American individual studying law must find out how the African deals with the law and use the MAAT process better to understand the dynamics of the American legal system to make sure that the feather is not heavier than the heart. They have turned into the spiritual and legal proceedings of the true God to weigh the correct system and lead others into the truth from an African spiritual balance.

To understand the meaning of the American justice system, the African Americans must understand the nature of the European if they are to combat them and deal with them on their legal procedures and law. Mandela stated, as I paraphrase what he said, is to deal with them, you must understand them and why they act the way they do and learn from their raghbat munkhafida (low desire) and nafs (self).

The American law does not fit Africans spiritual reasoning in their psyche. This creates an issue in the development of law and justice because African Americans' history concerning the justice system is flawed. Due to maltreatment over the years in their community, they are governed when dealing with the police. Distrust in the legal system when going to court over the year when many of them have not committed the crime but still are convicted in the court. During the trial, the system's makeup is stacked with individuals who do not understand the dynamics in their community but are chosen to be jurors and deciders of their fate.

Such as their community peers that do not live in the exact location but in the community on the other side of the track. Prejudice and malice in their heart when judging the circumstances. The law is not presented fair, and African Americans are often put in jail for lies and inadequate representation in the courtroom from a stacked testimony. Later, to be freed because the person lied when deciding the fate of the case for African Americans.

This is one or two of why the American legal system has been flawed, and the system seems to be failing the African American and disenfranchised communities. The American law does not care about any ethnic group. If it is not European, it is present in the decisions in the trial courts that sometimes do not make it to the appellate court due to lack of funds for the individuals in the court at the trial level.

This is another reason that the makeup of the courts and the criminal laws need to be looked at to be fair when it comes to certain crimes. Europeans have one rule for drug crimes than African Americans when time is being dispensed in the court.

One goes to rehab or a lesser charge to ensure they do not lose their children. While the other is punished, and their family is broken up and put in group homes and prison for years because the courts have deemed that the African American group is not worthy of being saved and are treated as savages.

The American legal system makes sure that the masses are blind to the social reasoning and the matters of law that govern their ability to think critically. This is pushed down to the churches, synagogues, temples, and mosques of their congregations, which are conditioned to keep the masses believing there is power in trusting the law. Once the people realize the detriment of the legal game, they will question the severity of the process of law.

If not thought out and challenged, I have found that the law will never change. The fundamental process of law will be accepted and never modified by unraveling the critical dimensions of the law and asking crucial social-political questions to answer simple things. The American rule is enclosed with only European's way of thinking using the African American female to help them keep the population in check. In Latin, the word *Vox Populi* (the opinions or beliefs of the majority) is that the truth according to the law and do they hear Vox Dei[1] if we would put it together Vox Populi, Vox Dei (Latin, 'the voice of the people is the voice of God').

If we are to understand the law and how justice should be developed according to the universal process. Then it is accumbent on the African American law students Male and Female to understand the system and how unfair it is towards our belief structure.

Once you have traveled back into Kemet to understand the nature of the soul and how it plays a critical part in your legal

---

[1]   Vox Dei – the voice of God

development. The ancestors will then speak to you and show you how and why you are wonderfully and mathematically astute and made according to your intelligence. Therefore, by tapping into your own spirit that is leading you into this greatness. Being a leader, lawyer, and child of thought.

By envisaging the dynamics of the law from each of these critical social groups and how American law has developed them into our legal system of justice. The ideas and the process were developed over some time and accepted in the country without help from African Americans during the founding of the country this is one of the greatest problems we will find in learning how to navigate the system.

We have as African Americans have adopted the skills and the abilities to understand the workings of the American legal system. But the critical problem we face is that they still control the courts and the legislation and policies in the states. Law attempts to bridge the theological gap from this perspective that came from theology these three theological theories Science of theology, Divisions of theology, Natural theology. When combining these processes into the system of law one must know the law and how it is shared.

It is critical that each student of law examine the true word and understand the epistemology of the legal system and the origin from where it was developed. Who were the actors, what were their thoughts, concerning the law and how does it play into the society in which we live?

NOTES

KNOWING HOW KEMET PLAYS A CRITICAL PART

T HE QUESTION THAT NEEDS to really be answered is what part Kemet plays in the equation for the understanding of the law. This is a very critical part of your knowledge in understanding the crucial points and aspects of law and the formation.

The Kemet people understood how-to live-in harmony with each other and follow the 42 Laws of MAAT. As a principle, Maat was developed to meet the complex needs of the emergent Egyptian state that embraced diverse peoples with conflicting interests. These rules sought to avert chaos, violence, and lies, expressed in the concept of Isfet[2]. By going back to find out how the original people Nubians dealt with the society it is incumbent on the African law student to better understand the mindset of the African and how they dealt with other nations.

This means that the Nubians understood the social and political process of law and how to govern others and create a peaceful nation with honor and respect. In the Karnak, temple you will the spiritual and social aspects of the knowledge of how they

---

[2]   Isfet or Asfet (meaning "injustice", "chaos", or "violence"; as a verb, "to do evil")

dealt with law and order. The Nubians came into Kemet to help assist the nation in building the pyramids and bring with them skilled laborers as well the architects. This helps you to better understand the nature of law and order the science of theology and how it is attached to the rule we follow today in the courtroom.

Everything has a meaning to it and the courtroom is filled with signs from ancient Kemet, when you study the makeup of the courtroom and walls you will see the scale which came from Anubis of how to judge if a person has done right from wrong and where they might go if the feather is heavier than the heart. Therefore, if the law is not just and the individuals are prompted to screw the results to keep a group down because they have an inner hatred of that group then the scales of justice might be flawed.

Therefore, it is very important to understand how to look at the inner soul of the situation and hear all the evidence to make sure a just verdict has been weighed correctly. The truth is always hind the lie, we must find that lie and bring it to light if we as law students are to be fair to our morals and soul in the courtroom. There are four critical processes that help us to deal with the procedures and keys to legal knowledge. C.A.P.S

Content- Grouping

Analysis—View

Process- the forces that affect our ideas and knowledge, politics, the economic, social, and psychological process to develop.

Systems- Interrelated

These are very important to the rule and order of any legal process by understanding the group on better understand their mindset, therefore earlier I introduced to you the **biopsychosocial** thoughts that many individuals miss in the justice system when dealing with different ethnic groups.

From there a critical process of viewing how they process the critical information in the court concerning their action is also very crucial. **Forensic psychology** plays a very important part in the courtroom at the time of hearings if justice is to be rendered for the defendant. The investigation and the truth must be investigated to uncover the lie.

Then the legal **process** can then begin to determine the severity of the crime or issue that the defendant may face. If these steps are not realized and just because one case speaks to the condition of the current case the psychology of the case might be different and an unjust ruling will be entered against a defendant.

Each of these actions is critical in dealing with and determining the case law is understanding the crime and finding out the truth from the lie, it comes from the moral and spiritual understanding of the conditions and positions of how society has developed the people in it. The laws that are used to govern the legal side help to shape our thinking but if the ones judging the situation are flawed then many innocent individuals might be put in jail or say incarcerated because of a guilty heart and knowledge of that group.

There is a psychology to the understanding of the law and not only is Kemet needed to be in the equation how we view others and live among each other is critical in the scope of care. As a student of law, it will be your responsibility to view each case with respect and dignity as if it was you being tried in the courtroom God is watching and recording.

WHAT HAVE YOU BEEN TAUGHT?

W HAT HAVE YOU BEEN taught will affect what you believe to be the truth when dealing with the law and how you see the people you encounter within the courtroom?

As a law student to understand the nature of the law is to know the people in each community by visiting the areas and having a rapport with them. This helps you to gain a legal perspective on the pulse of that community and analysis for yourself the problems they have been facing that are causing the crimes in that area.

Being proactive and understanding the people's actions is critical to making a lasting effect in the justice system, waiting for the crime in these communities to get out of control and judging them is a failure. Forward-thinking and focused groups help to create a better society by figuring out how to mitigate the problems before it creates death in the communities.

This probably has never been thought of and used in the law schools nor taught to you by any professor. But if you have ever been to Kemet, not only will you gain a sense of respect for self you will understand the three social developments that move the social needle. **SSS**

Self-esteem
Self-respect
Self-development

This moves into a very critical part of the legal perspective and balance according to the rule of the Kemet thought process. Which are even deeper to the spiritual and moral portions of your legal soul.

Values
Integrity
Principles

If you do not have any of these characteristics in your spirit and being then doing the right thing will become fussy and following the rule of law will become difficult. You need to search your own soul and process each of these critical concepts while you are in law school. If the Europeans train you to hate yourself then you will reflect that in the courtroom during cases against your own people. Not because you want to but because you were trained to dismiss the three basic tenements (**SSS**)[3].

How does a system make you hate yourself and believe you can conform to their system of justice? While you reject your own development and people this is a dangerous position to be in called a confused state. God did not require that you assimilate your captor that is called **Stockholm syndrome** if you can be trained to hate your own people what do you think they will do to you when it is your time.

Therefore, suddenly in the current news, you find a senate that is already going against placing the first African American sister

---

[3]   **Self-esteem**
Self-respect
Self-development

on the bench. God is standing by to show them what you trained might realize there need to be some changes, and the only way the nation can see that he exists is to put her in place. Belove remember in Kemet, women also were kings and queens that helped to rule our nation then and now.

What you have been taught is critical to your survival and outcome if you have a Kemet mindset to realize God and the ancestors are calling you to order and showing you that everything that was taught to you is needed to adapt and control the new destiny. We are pilgrims in a foreign land the scriptures are correct the bible is opening to speak to us from Kemet concerning our contributions to civilization from the valley of the kings and queen[4].

It is understanding self and how information is taught to us that freedom is contained the schools that we have attended, and the development of the knowledge has to be reevaluated and challenged to free the mind, soul, and spirit of our training.

Or we will be walking repositories of a slave master's knowledge and be misguided and forgetful of our own accomplishments and undertake the mindset of our captor. That is why Truthfully, we have had a hard time grasping the true beauty of Kemet and how the Nubians created the contributions to civilization. We have been trained to forget our land and African past and assume and assimilate that the United States legal system has us in mind. Unless the keepers of the law on the constitution are not challenged and the laws truly added us in the distribution of the stolen wealth off our backs then we will never get a fair shake. The pursuit of liberty and justice for all will still make you believe you are property.

---

[4]   Four https://ikgculturalresourcecenter.com/study-tour-in-egypt

Therefore, when they do the same crime, it seems that the laws shield them from the same justice, they call law. they teach you in law school that the is the law of the land and everyone must follow it but every time you go to court you see justice perverted and African Americans and the disenfranchised are punished.

Therefore, what do you believe is created in the mind of the African American law student when it comes to the belief that the law is fair. How do you dispense justice through a system that is created to spare the children of the creators of the law and punish those who follow the rules made by the captors, Kemet helps us to search deeper into the spiritual abilities and judge according to the laws given by divine presence?

Once you lose the respect of yourself and replace it with confusion it will be hard to navigate the road from a lie. Tapping into the Kemet process and understanding how it was taught will help you to come back in alignment with the universe and see the spiritual side of your inner being it will change how you process what you have been taught. Regardless of how it we revealed to us through the Prizm of others and what they want to believe concerning your faith and your witness.

What if you have been believing a lie so long and you find out that everything you learned was built off that lie, which and really it was hidden from you. Then one day you find out the truth. But the system wanted you to continue with the lie to conform with the social structure and legal precedence because it would cause an economic shift in the capitalistic environment and the court. Remember that the African's follow the spiritual model and the Europeans follow the profit development of the same lateral pyramid upside down.

If we are to crack the egg, then we must retrain how we are taught in the schools of the Europeans and train the masses.

Or we will produce and promote useless containers of thinkers in our communities. Not leaders and critical people with a deep history of accomplishments o civilizations.

Therefore, you see a great number of churches being targeted because God Is not pleased with the way training is being conducted. The structures that are intended to help the communities are being robbed from within and exposed because the people who are priests have not followed the law of God. In the Bible within Hosea[5], God said that he will deal with the priest who failed the people.

In your education and knowledge, we must begin to understand the stuff we were taught to deal with the status quo the courts and the society have shared with African American students and lawyers. If the truth of the word and the law books are to line up, we are to live in a just society.

Then the student must go back into Kemet and study the truth and realize there was truth on the walls that showed the world how to govern but somehow, they perverted that sacred power and turned the law into a lie. Some of the information was changed to fit the needs of the Europeans and take from the history of the African and make it there's.

It is the duty of the African American student studying law to investigate and understand the truth and follow the signs. If they are to better understand the system of justice and combat the mess, we are in.

When you have been mis-educated and the light is cut on from the lies told to you in not only law school from the theories and application but from the application of the justice and laws how

---

[5]   Hosea 4: 7 the more the priest increased, the more they sinned against me; they exchanged their Glory for something disgraceful.

they were developed. This becomes critical and concerning while navigating the structure of the foundations of the law and the books.

It is incumbent on you as a student of research to investigate and find out the truth of self and knowledge that has been kept from you and twisted. The only reason many African Americans fail law school is that the establishment does not want them in law school.

It is not that they cannot understand the dynamics of the lessons. It is because when they find out the origin of the structure of law, it will then help to create a balance in the legal system and a shift in the power structure.

NOTE:

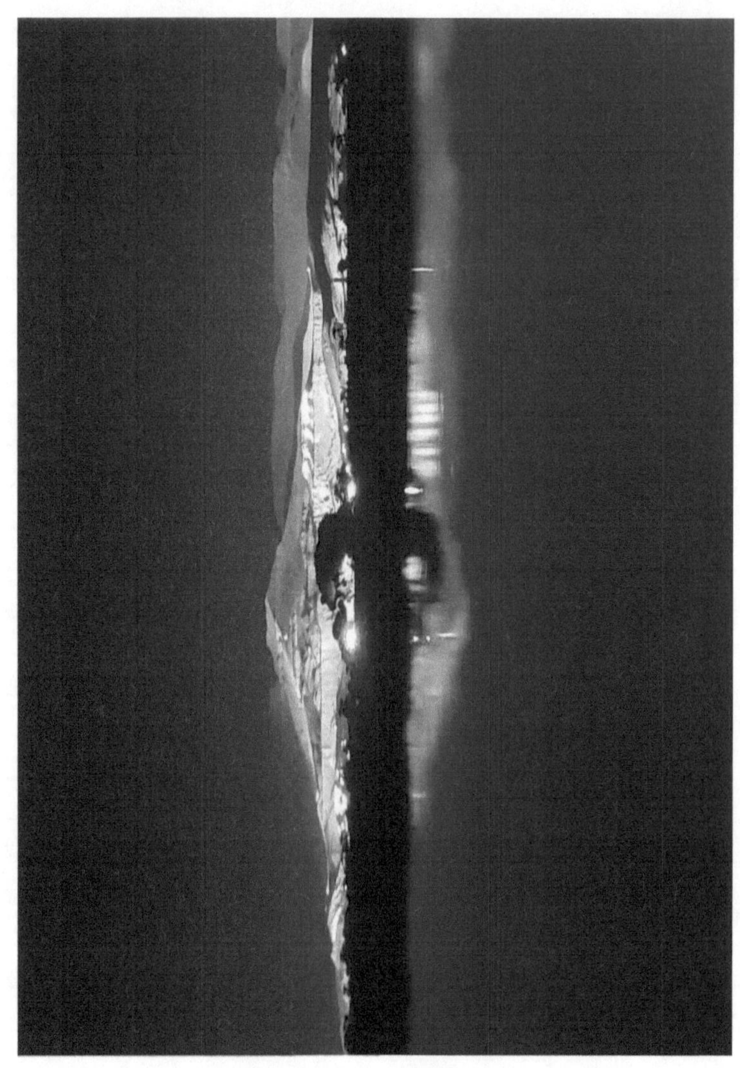

Valley of the Kings

HOW CAN YOU CONTROL
THE SYSTEM?

THE ONLY WAY TO control the system is to begin to campaign for the legislative seats and change some of the laws that govern the communities and situations. Then creating a better understanding of the legal system and curriculum in the law schools that deal with the society that everyone lives in this will be the only way to gain control of the justice system.

If the overhaul of the system is not done according to the dynamics of the society in which we all live. Then the laws and the operation of the laws will still be an issue in the law schools and the justice department when dealing with the processes and the procedures of the criminal and legal system.

If the legal minds of our nation want to change, then the way the justice system has used the art of control and laws will have to reflect the society and how it is used to govern and correct the behavior of the people in each community. It must fit the needs and the social-economic background of the people.

To deal with the control factor moral dialogue must be one of the forefront thoughts when dealing with law and justice. The real issues that I have found it social communication and articulate motions to address the legal problems in the communities which also must be thought of when dealing with control and law.

Who will the end results help and how will they accomplish the social-economic conditions in the world of social justice and legal precedence in our community in America? How will the African American law student deal with the power structure that is evidently European and their thinking towards sharing legal power is only granted in their social-economic construct and legal thoughts to hold on to the control and power of the law?

Many of these critical thoughts must be dealt with in law school and how the curriculum is formed and trained in the law schools. By dealing with this critical and crucial matter it will have a profound impact on the legal system and cause an economic and mental problem that must be fully understood in each community.

By going back into the epistemological concepts of law and finding out the origin of the code of law and who created the true balance for the community and society it will help the thinking of the student. To make a more decisive decision when it comes to **legal precedence** and **procedures**. The law needs to be envisaged through the lens of each ethnic thought if it is to be an American thought not just a European model, derived from profits and incarceration.

Therefore, the highest court the **Supreme Court** must be balanced with not only European men and women. It must include African American females who understand hopefully the plight of their community and social issues. This may be a bad thing if the pick is from a tokenism position and put in a high place to help keep the power structure in place and control the masses.

If the justice system is so embedded with the European thoughts and legal system methods that are derived from common law, then the law will always be flawed and unfair and never balanced. Law when it is conducted correctly envisages the social conditions of all citizens especially the African American community in ways by understanding the effectiveness of the individuals who participate and are involved within the community.

Law students must take time out to challenge the status quo and ask questions as to the validity of the charges and if they fit the social norms. When understanding the conditions that many African Americans face within the African American community. The legal minds of the law student must know what role they should play is to help curve the social issues if the norms are out of bounce.

Therefore, the student of law must make critical observations of how the law is used, and how its power of influence, is given when engaging the religious leaders in the community. This entails exploring the civic and community involvement, attitudes, and social changes in the African American community, which influence both the African American community.

Therefore, when including everyone at the table of reasons, the research can then further examine the neighborhoods associated with poverty and poor living conditions by trying to understand why some areas in the city higher levels of incarceration have than do other similar areas within the same city/community.

Who will control the power and the justice in the communities or will the law that has forced the African American and the disenfranchised be forever subjected to the abuse of the European legal system and a failed justice model?

Who holds the power and control of the justice system will it ever be fair and just in the society to which we live and represent? How can we crack the egg and keep law and order in an unjust legal system created by the slaveholders during the time of the writing of the constitution and declaration of independence? The law student when in law school must take the steps to deal with the thoughts of the framers and decide if they really wanted to have a just society outside of slavery.

Most of this was done during the change of slavery and there were no African Americans there to interject anything in the constitution to make it a fail binding matter. If the law was to be governed and applied for all citizens, then the African Americans should have been invited not later to follow the law that was already against them.

The Africans who came over on the ships were very intelligent and could have contributed to the founding of the constitution and gave the individuals who were kicked out of England some pointers.

Therefore, it is still time to deal with the law of the land and deal with the social inequities of the times we are faced within the shores of America to balance the legal system. The system that tells you one thing but goes against their own laws to keep power for Europeans in the legal system is something that has been shared in every nation where Africans have been developed.

The law student when using critical thinking must deal with the social construct of the law and understand the true meaning. The law is for everyone who is to be born on the shores of the United States but somehow, they keep on debating the law on voting and asking for the right to vote.

The law students and others who follow the law believe in the process and so-called fairness of the system but for some reason the laws and the application are flawed. Until change comes then the same laws will apply to the citizens to which it is intended to help.

BETRAYED BY THE CAUSE OF JUSTICE?

T O DEAL WITH THE issues of law and how it works a deeper dive must be conducted towards how our democracy is formed and applied to the nation. First by seeking out the rights in the system that is unfair to the citizens to which the law applies. Ancillary, the justice system must investigate how the power is distributed and dispensed to the legal system of the United States and all territories.

There has been no redress from the courts for individuals who came from and through slavery only to be told that the system is there for them which is a lie. The benefits and the rights were only given to the Europeans and all light skin fair individuals who came to the country and the ones that were enslaved and brought were denied the same benefits.

Many of the African Americans who were born inside of the United States has still not received fair and equal treatment under the laws that were set forth. They must still fight, protest, and cry to a government to deal with the adjustment of liberty and the pursuit of the tree of life. The power structure and education of the laws in the schools and the educational requirements even in law school who continually finds ways to disqualify many African American black males for the process.

The laws that have been enacted have failed the marginalized and disenfranchised. The slave plantation mindset has still been applied to the legal system and the people who were affected by the process and laws in a democratic egalitarianism manner must deal with the social and political problems which the legal system has produced.

This has caused an unconscious psychological condition that focuses on legislation and education that need to be addressed to deal with the law and how it was disseminated to the communities and society in which we live.

The system of law and the fundamentals of the process in the justice system must grapple with what they have forced the people primality African Americans both male and female particularly of the injustice done to them because of the laws and legacy through slavery. This breakdown of justice and social unrest in the legal system has betrayed the cause of justice and created segregation of the legal proceedings of economic and educational means of fairness.

The betrayal is conducted in the laws set in motion to keep a group from ever rising in a mass against the wishes of the majority to stay in power. This may be one of the cases that the laws have created a second-class environment for citizens by using the law and the constitution to hold others at bay because of their hearts condition and evil built up with malice.

We have been betrayed by the justice system and the laws and the training of the law is only helping keep Europeans in power in the sense of the law. Yes, the law is to be fair for the people in the communities and it seems as though sometimes it is fair.

But many times, in our society we find just the opposite of the law and many disturbing cases of brutality and fake information given in the courtroom when the judge knows the truth but still allows the prosecutor to present untrue information in a trial.

We can go back to Emmitt Till[6] and his trial in 1955 informs us that the law was perverted and unjust. Emmitt Till was a fourteen-year-old boy, who had been brutally murdered and his body thrown in the Tallahatchie River, but despite clear evidence that two white men committed the crime, an all-white jury returned a "Not Guilty" verdict after just an hour of deliberation.

So where was this justice in the land when the court fully knew that the crime was committed and even today the courts and the justice system have individuals in it who still pervert the law of the land and betray the trust of the people in the communities? The African American trained lawyers try to defend the sanctity of the legal system and make it fair, but they must remember the law was not geared to help the former slaves and the other people who were not here during the construction of the declaration and constitution.

Therefore, what we have is a legal system that needs to be fair and practical to the citizens of the United States.

Just envisage and **exculpate** this case, Central Park Five[7] in the 1980s, if you believe that the law has been fair to many African Americans in this society. The law enforcement quickly apprehended five juveniles — four of them black and one Hispanic — and tried them for assault, robbery, rape, riot, sexual abuse, and attempted murder. The confessions of the

---

6   The Emmett Till Murder Trial: An Account (famous-trials.com)

7   The Central Park Five: Boys Wrongly Convicted By A Racist System (allthatsinteresting.com)

Central Park Five were the only semblance of evidence police had at their disposal to lock the teenagers up — confessions the group later said were coerced. All five of them received sentences ranging from five to 15 years, much of which they served, even **after the truth** had been revealed to **lawmakers** and the public alike.

Each of these critical cases is just a clear indication of the law at work for the people and it is the duty of the African American students to make sure that the law is fair, and it does not betray their oath as officers of the court. Nor be led to follow the laws that hold innocent people in jail because they want to go along with the Europeans and kind favor in the justice system.

Now the critical questions that arise for each case and the law of the nation are how they prosecute the individuals who govern the law when they have blatantly misrepresented the laws. Elizabeth Lederer, the lead prosecutor in the Central Park jogger case, resulted in the wrongful conviction of five black and Latino boys. This shows us that the law can be manipulated to fit the needs so of the justice system.

Therefore, it is critical and crucial for the African American student in law to understand the nature of the law and how to apply it to the situation and make sure that if they have a case then it is fair and just.

UNFAIR LAWS IN A JUST SOCIETY

I N AN UNJUST SOCIETY, how do you navigate through the rough waters of the legal system and keep loving a country that has used its laws to keep many people from assisting in the development of the country?

The laws that were enacted must fit the needs of the people this is one of the most crucial and critical parts of the law. The student must understand the meaning of the issues and apply the law of the land with a precise application if the legal system is to be fair for everyone.

Therefore, what we keep finding is that the laws are unfair and not just in the society and when the law student is grappling with the reason and how to fit it to the truth then they are confused with how the law is working and for who.

When law students, primarily African Americans better understand the issues that have caused their communities such dire conditions because of the passing of some constitutional laws. They will better acknowledge the problems once they investigate the severity of the minds of the framers when they decided on the law for African Americans. Structural racism is one of the most fundamental concerns of the changing of the laws in the nation. It keeps many African American communities down and in the same place as they have been in thirty years only to move up probably 5% percent if any.

The **Dred Scott** case told the nation that the writing of the constitution and amendments were rubber stamps when concerning African Americans in society. The laws promising to give free blacks land and protection in the law were not true. There are many insistences, where the law has failed African Americans and others in society. How can the system be fair if the laws that govern the justice system are not geared to assist every citizen in the United States?

We are in some bad legal times and the system must be challenged if the wrongs in the constitution will be changed and corrected to give relief to the downcast. A legal forensic audit must be conducted of the law system and reevaluated if there are to be any changes to this system. The justice system needs an overhaul and a legal makeover if there is justice in an unfair legal system. The African American and other liked minded law students must develop a critical thinking tank in the law school to investigate the constitution and reevaluate the meaning of the framers if there will be any conclusive critical legal changes to the mentality of the rule of law.

The question that must be asked is what the rule of law is and for whom does it apply to in a just society. The process of res-judicata[8] indicates that the constitution is built upon this very act and fact. If this is the case and the system is already developed on this basis then the difficulty will be changing the social construct of the law to fit the masses.

This is one of the critical thinking processes we need to investigate and comb through if the law is to be fair in an unjust society. This is one of the critical and crucial reasons that

---

[8]   The thing has been decided

the 15th amendment is critical to the conversation and thought process.

…The final decision of Congress not to include anything relating to the right to vote in the Fourteenth Amendment, aside from the provisions of section 2,[1] left the issue of Black suffrage solely with the states, and Northern states were generally as loath as Southern to grant the ballot to African Americans, both the newly freed and those who had never been slaves.[2] But, in the second session of the 39th Congress, the right to vote was extended to African Americans by statute in the District of Columbia and the territories, and the seceded states as a condition of readmission had to guarantee Black suffrage…[9]

…The Fifteenth Amendment, it announced, did not confer the right . . . [to vote] upon anyone, but merely invested the citizens of the United States with a new constitutional right which is . . . exemption from discrimination in the exercise of the elective franchise on account of race, color, or previous condition of servitude.[1] But in subsequent cases, the Court, conceding that this article has originally been construed as giving no affirmative right . . . to vote and as having been designed primarily to prevent discrimination, professed to be able to see that under some circumstances it may operate as the immediate source of a right to vote.

In all cases where the former slave-holding States had not removed from their **Constitutions the words** 'white man' as a qualification for voting, this provision did, in effect, confer on him the right to vote, because . . . it annulled the discriminating word white, and this left him in the enjoyment of the same right as white persons. **And such would be the effect of any future**

---

[9]   Right to Vote Clause: Doctrine and Practice | Constitution Annotated | Congress.gov | Library of Congress

constitutional provision of a State which would give the right of voting exclusively to white people. . .[10]

Although the immediate concern of the Amendment was to guarantee to the emancipated slaves the right to vote, the Amendment is cast in fundamental terms, terms transcending the controversy, and grants protection to all persons, not just members of a particular race.

All this sounds great, but the laws were still benefiting the masses of the individuals who wrote the constitution and the amendments. Still, the laws student must investigate who of African American descent was in the room when they drafted this document and legislation. The laws are there, and the language was created but the problem even today in the law school is that the laws are only governing European thought process that was adopted from England. Knowing this question is why only it is the basis of legal thought.

Remember that real thoughts came from the legal mind of the Africans who were **Nubians** and developers of the pyramids in ancient Africa known as **Kemet**. This is where the original thoughts came from, and it was here they recreated the modalities from the Africans to fit their society and crossed up the truth therefore they do not want many African American laws students to matriculate into the **jurisprudence** law school part.

Once in the school of law, you can then realize the social changes to the original laws, and it will question to your legal mind the truth and how justice should be formed and administered to society and the world.

---

[10]   Critical information that was in the 15th amendment that needs to be studied and ratified, lawyers using words that many African Americas and citizens did not fully understand at the time of the drafting.

NOTE

IN THE MIDST OF ADVERSITY

I T THE MIDST OF adversaries we have overcome and adapted to the situations life we live. The system of law and the structure of justice is not fair towards the so-called African American who has been brought to the shores of America. Through adversary and the misinterpretation of the legal understanding concerning law has created a detriment to the social justice problem.

This is the reason why African American law students need to better understand how to deal with the law and the structure of the United States within the scope of the law. The African American community and the church have always navigated the communities through the political, social, and economic conditions that many of the people in the communities find distasteful emotionally and psychologically.

Each community must take on a different mission to deal with the social conditions. The groups, churches, synagogues, temples, and mosques must be looked at to teach the people in the communities how to deal with not only the challenges found in the status quo. The law student, preachers, and individuals in the church must take on the concerns of the community by dealing with the ambiguous events that cause difficulty in the communities by resolving the problem that needs to be addressed concerning the law.

The greatest issue plaguing African American law students is the dissemination of critical information which will help them to reconstruct how they deal with the social construct of the justice system and challenge the thoughts of the Europeans. Therefore, the action plan is to research and understand the nature of the conditions by engaging the critical issues of the communities where the disenfranchised live in the world by trying to change the mindset of the justice system and by addressing questions and issues significant for those who have been affected.

Law students must envisage the cases that have been decided to better understand the nature of the justice presented in the cases and learn from mistakes during sentencing each of these issues and situations must be understood while learning about the experience and history of the people who share the same lived situations.

The African American law student's problem with the church today is that the leadership no longer understands the people who they serve, the pastors do not know the community, and the community really does not know the heart and mind of the justice system anymore these days. The problem that has caused the communities to fail is that the leadership has not addressed the communities' social issues and just allowed them to go on day-by-day.[11]

We find a justice system using a complication of legal laws to create a justice system in the United States. The framers of the law were slaveholders and did not want to give up power to the enslaved or anyone who came into the country. The laws were

____

[11]   Gavin, K (2015) PROCESS ACTION PROJECT: ON THE AFRICAN AMERICAN COMMUNITY IN ROCKDALE TX, p.34

only to fit the social construct of Europeans and keep others out who were of a darker hue. Over time the amendments were developed to offset the original laws but still found ways to exclude the same people out of the rights and liberty of the states and country regardless of the framer's thoughts.

Those thoughts were of the mindset that only European individuals will have the land and control the processes in the country. It is through these adversarial processes that these laws and the justice system must be changed to give everyone the same rights and benefits to the American dream if it is to be fair. Regardless of the problems, it has caused to many of the disenfranchised individuals who have still adapted and overcame the obstacles set in their way by trusting in a system not meant for them but eternal in heaven.

The law schools must teach the students how to understand the true nature of law and how it is to govern the masses who need to follow the law of the land. It must be fair and show impartiality when decided not biased and one-sided only to fit the European mindset. It is ironic that the same laws that are used in the justice system are the ones that the African Americans and others still believe in regardless of the situations and methods used against them to keep them down and they are the ones who have upheld the truths of the law.

Through the midst of adversary and the bending of the laws God whom we serve has kept the disinherited from being used and abused too long. The law and the justice system that was developed to hold the masses down is challenged in the hearts and the mind of the people who have been affected the most to still believe in the greatness of the possibilities of the nation in which they live.

They can chain your body and keep you out of the process, but the freedom comes when the power of God through our ancestors comes alive to challenge the process and speak to us from the spiritual world through our development. During adversary, the soul searches for the truth and when it begins to lead us back to self and determination it will help to realign the situations and show us how to deal with our conditions.

When the masses begin to understand the power of the concepts of nature and how the God you call on enters the situation the balance of the scales and your heart will be lifted. In the feather heavier than your heart. Or is the heart lighter than the feather, study to show yourself approved to do the work know the structure of the law, and make the change to challenge the wrongs?

CRITICAL THINKING IN CONCERNING LAW

Voting Rights and Equal Protection Based on Race and National Origin

MANY SECTORS OF OUR society, especially Black and Latino Americans, Indigenous families, and men without property, have not been accorded full citizenship rights. No issue has been more profoundly disturbing than race in the development of U.S. constitutional law. None of the infinite arrays of distinctions drawn by U.S. governments in nearly two centuries has been more vital and controversial than race discrimination. Some of the blatant injustices are so magnanimous as to defy human comprehension. The current Justice Robert's Court continues to issue rulings that inflict harm to our democracy and has once again struck a devastating blow to the nation's best strategic defense against racial voter suppression. Reconfiguring the rules of our democracy to make it more difficult to vote is one of the central legacies of the Roberts court.

The *Voting Rights Act of 1965* was delivered on the proclaimed ideals of the founding fathers' philosophical belief that "we are all" created equal. The model of freedom and opportunity that motivated the creation of the Constitution reflects the spiritual strength of a nation. Today, that assumption for many lingers by a thread, and our nation's spiritual, moral compass requires a much-needed adjustment.

Slavery was constitutional before the adoption of the *13th Amendment* in 1865. There was no promise of *equal protection* under the Constitution and no limits on *race discrimination* before adopting the *14th Amendment*. However, despite the majestic words of the Declaration of Independence that "*all men are created equal,*" people of color in America were anything but equal under the U.S. Constitution. Courts enforced the institution of slavery consistently by ruling in favor of slave owners and against blacks. The judiciary enforced the *fugitive slave clause* and blocked northern states from providing aid and protection to blacks who escaped from slavery. In *Prigg v. Pennslyvania,* the Court declared a state law that prevented the use of violence or force to remove any person from the State to return the individual to slavery unconstitutional. The *Fugitive Slave Act* adopted by the second Congress required that jurists produce blacks who escaped from slavery.

Constitutional amendments known as the *post-civil war amendments* were directly associated with liberating former slaves in captivity and granting their fundamental civil rights. The 15th Amendment declares: *The right of the citizenry of the U.S. to vote cannot be withheld by the U.S. or by any state on behalf of race, color, or previous condition of servitude.*" However, these amendments fell short of ending the challenges of former slaves, and their rights continued to face restrictions by black codes of many southern white states. *Black codes* were rigid state and local laws intended to establish systems of peonage reflecting slavery.

These codes were legal for whites to put blacks into indentured servitude, remove *voting rights,* and seize children for labor.

Gradually, the black regulation codes were overturned, followed by federal civil rights legislation passed during the *Reconstruction* era. However, the Supreme Court's 1896 ruling in *Plessy v. Ferguson* that *separate but equal* doctrine underlying segregation was constitutional essentially abolished the *14th Amendment* for the newly freed blacks. The Court said in a 7 to 1 vote that *"a state law that implies a legal discrepancy among the races does not violate the 13th Amendment forbidding involuntary servitude, nor does it tend to reestablish such a condition."*

Consensus gradually developed as the 20th century progressed that segregation was morally wrong. In *Brown v. Board of Education,* the Court's 1954 decision on anti-segregation, though a lightning bolt o the Court eclipsed bringing much change over southern white establishment policies of mass resistance. However, it was not until the *1964 Civil Rights Act* and the *1965 Voting Rights Act* under President Lyndon Johnson did the federal government finally execute the ideals of the Constitution declared in 1788. The first three words, *"We the People,"* affirm that the government exists to serve all its citizens.

Nevertheless, today in multiple southern states, those ideals hang by a thread with *voter suppression bills* based on discrimination being passed by state legislatures into law. Texas joins Georgia, Florida, and sixteen other states that have passed *voter suppression laws* in 2021 in direct response to voters of color using their authority at the polls to demand change, transparency, and accountability. The state-by-state efforts to suppress the *right to vote* aided by the Supreme Court's decision in *Shelby County v. Holder* and *Brnovich v. DNC* have severely diminished the protections expressed in the *Voting Rights Act.* The Court held in *Brnovich v. DNC* that Arizona's out of precinct policy and H.B. 2023 did not breach Section 2 of the Voting Rights Act, and H.B. 2023 was not implemented with discriminatory motives. The Senate has failed to enact the *For the People Act* (H.R. 1) and the *John Lewis Voting Rights Advancement Act* (H.R. 4) to effectively redirect the zeitgeist of *voter suppression* currently sweeping across the nation.

Shelby County v. Holder: Section 4. b and Section 5

In 2013, *Shelby County v. Holder,* a county from Alabama, argued that *Section 4. b* and *Section 5* of the VRA were unconstitutional. *Section 4. b* included the formula used to identify the target jurisdictions; a history of *Jim Crow-era* policies was a vital component of the procedure. Section 5 required specific jurisdictions to submit all voting law changes to the Department of Justice or a federal court for review, known as preclearance. *Chief Justice John Roberts,* writing the majority opinion, ruled that the aggressive preemptive measures crucial to ensuring the black vote were no longer warranted because *"they had worked so well."* The majority opinion essentially rolled back the Voting Rights Act's protections and permitted states to change their *voting protocols* without outside oversight and accountability. However, previously in 2010, in *Shelby County v. Holder,* Shelby County, Alabama sued *Attorney General Eric Holder* in D.C. federal court, arguing certain aspects of the Voting Rights Act were unconstitutional. A district judge disagreed, ruling that the act would stay in place. The *Court of Appeals* affirmed.

The Court's reasoning in 2013 fell apart rapidly as Republicans quickly moved to implement a *voter I.D. law* that created a particular hardship on black voters. A federal appeals court ruling held that the new law specifically targeted voters of color with laser precision. *Sherilynn Ifill,* NAACP president and director-counsel of the *Legal Defense and Educational Fund* in lower Manhattan, asserts "that once the bonds of *Section 5* were released, the rest of the country learned from the South how to enact *voter suppression strategies.*" A wave of *voter suppression* tactics including *voter I.D. laws, gerrymandering,* and skillfully crafted *election changes* have steadily deteriorated the *VRA* over the past several years in states nationwide, including Wisconsin, Kansas, and Indiana.

Republicans have now adopted a blueprint of the *white supremacy discrimination* strategies that had permeated the corrupt State of Mississippi during the Jim Crow era. *Jim Crow laws* were a collection of local and state statutes that legalized *racial segregation.* The laws, which existed for about a century from post-civil war until 1968, were designed to marginalize blacks by preventing them the *right to vote*, obtain an education, hold employment, housing, and other opportunities afforded to whites. Those who defied Jim Crow laws faced fines, arrest, jail, violence, lynchings, and death.

The *Voting Rights Act,* seen as the bellwether of the civil rights movement, was strictly implemented to ensure that no citizen would be denied the right to vote due to color or race by creating a coverage formula for political subdivisions and states with a history of enduring discriminatory practices against black voting populations. A common form of discrimination included literacy tests given to poor whites and blacks with devices like Mississippi's soap bubble test requiring black voters to guess the number of bubbles in a bar of soap to have to vote. In 1865, in *Guinn v. United States,* the Court asserted unconstitutional a literacy test for voting that contained a *grandfather clause* that exempted from the requirement all who could vote, along with their descendants. The blatant motivation was to exclude blacks wishing to vote while providing an exception that benefited whites only.

The VRA was established to impede discriminatory devices by requiring those districts to submit any new changes in *voting procedures, including closing or moving polling places, reduced voting days, requirements for more limited forms of identification, and purges to voting rolls* to the district court in Washington, D.C. or the Justice Department for approval before they enacted them known as *preclearance*. Kevin Morris, a sociology doctoral student, recently testified this summer before Congress in support of the John Lewis Voting Rights Act. His testimony on research at the *Brennan Center for Law and Justice* at *NYU Law School* demonstrates the discrimination facing ethnic and racial minorities after the Supreme Court's decision in the 2013 *Shelby County v. Holder* decision that struck down the *preclearance condition* of the 1965 Voting Rights Act.

The preclearance condition was reauthorized by the legislature every few years through early 2000. However, in the decade since the formula outlined in which district fell under its mandate was struck down, many states have changed their selecting outlined in how setting outlined in, voting practices in discriminatory ways and impact. The *John Lewis Voting Rights Act* proposes an updated revision to the formula and would bring back the preclearance condition. Morris asserts that passing the act would avoid suing each time a state enacts repressive, discriminatory measures. Morris suggests that litigation is costly, time-consuming, and can only be done most often after a bill goes into effect. In finding the act unconstitutional and ending the preclearance requirement for the covered counties and states, *Chief Justice John Roberts* declared that *"the blight of racial discrimination in voting, a constitutional right of the 15th Amendment that had infected the electoral process in our nation for a century,"* and which the act was designed to correct was alleviated in 2013. Suggesting that the VRA was no longer necessary because it had succeeded prior did not reflect the truth in many covered districts nationwide. It strongly suggested otherwise. Justice Ruth B. Ginsburg understood that the VRA was a wall holding a whole press of difficulties at bay. As a justice in the minority vote, Ginsburg knew that she could not prevent the eradication of the VRA. She devised an analogy of such concise magnitude that all who heard it understood the importance of keeping the act in place. Ginsburg asserts, *"throwing out preclearance when it has functioned and continues to operate to eradicate discriminatory changes is like tossing your umbrella in a rainstorm just because you are not getting wet."*

A Fundamental Right Under Equal Protection

"I think it is attributable to a phenomenon called perpetuation of racial entitlement. Whenever a society adopts racial entitlements, it is difficult to get out of them through the normal political process." Supreme Court Justice Anthony Scalia

The Supreme Court has regularly declared that the *right to vote* is a fundamental right protected under *equal protection* established in *Harper v. Virginia* (1966), *Kramer v. Union Free School District* (1969), and *Reynolds v. Sims* (1964). The right to vote is regarded as essential because it is vital in a democracy. In a democracy, society through voting allows the citizens to choose their elected officials and government while making them accountable. The 15th Amendment precludes denial of the right to vote on race or previous condition of servitude. Race discrimination regarding voting also receives strict scrutiny under the *equal protection clause* of the *14th Amendment,* as a racial classification and as an apparent infringement of the fundamental right to vote in our nation. The Court emphasized denial of equal protection in *Gomillion v. Lightfoot* when city borders were redrawn to ostracize black voters. Tuskegee, Alabama, redesigned its boundaries that changed its geographical shape from a square to a twenty-eight-sided figure. All black voters were positioned outside the city with apparent racial bias; thus, the districting was declared unconstitutional, outlined in *Hunter v. Underwood.*

The Supreme Court has determined that the fundamental right to vote with freedom for the candidate of one's choosing is of the very essence of a society that is democratic. Any restrictions on that basic right strike at the core of representative government. Thus, *"any unjustified discrimination in determining who may participate in government affairs or the selection of government officials undermines the legitimacy of a representative government"* established in *Kramer v. Union Free School District*. Therefore, any unjustified racial bias in determining who may participate in political affairs or selecting government officials also undermines the legitimacy of representative government.

The Court has long stated that the right to vote is a *"basic political right because it is a preservative of all rights"* outlined in *Yick Wo. v. Hopkins*. Voting is a form of expression, but it is also how all citizens choose a government to safeguard their interests and liberties. The Court observed that *"no rights are more valuable in a country than having a voice in the election of those who legislate the laws under which as good citizens, we must live.* Even fundamental rights are illusory if the *right to vote* is undermined, as established in *Westberry v. Sanders*.

Thus, laws that establish infringement on the right to vote that require meeting strict scrutiny. The Supreme Court has explained in *Harper v. Virginia St. Bd. of Elections* that *"since the right to exercise the franchise in a freely unimpaired manner is preservative of other basic political and civil rights, any alleged infringement of the right of citizens to vote must be carefully and meticulously scrutinized."*

In reviewing cases, three types of government restrictions can be identified in the many cases regarding voting rights. The first examines laws that deny some citizens the right to vote. Second, consider dilutions of the voting power. Third, it examines inequalities in counting votes as a denial of equal protection and focuses on the Court's landmark decision in *Bush v. Gore*. The Court ruled 5 to 4 *per curiam* opinion that counting the uncounted ballots without standards denies equal protection.

Some cases examine racial discrimination concerning voting. Many of the restrictions on voting have been intended to limit voting by blacks. Finally, some cases focus on laws that restrict the availability of candidates and parties to have access to the ballot, excessive filing fee requirements, gerrymandering motivated by race, deviations from majority rule, photo identification requirements, residency requirements, and poll taxes.

At large, elections and multimember districts also have a significant discriminatory effect. If a city using at large elections has a white majority and has a pattern of racially polarized voting, what results will be that no black will be elected when blacks are a significant minority in that district. The Court has determined that *at large voting schemes and multimember jurisdictions usually minimize the voting power of blacks and Latinos by allowing the political majority to elect all representatives of a given jurisdiction.* Any law that excludes a racial minority from voting is declared unconstitutional as denying *equal protection.*

In *Nixon v. Herndon,* the Court rejected a Texas law that excluded black from voting in primary elections. When the State tried to stop holding primary elections, it delegated the task to private businesses and the political parties. The Court declared that this also was unconstitutional and ruled that because the parties were executing a public function, they were tasked with meeting *equal protection* requirements.

Constitutional Provisions Protecting the Right to Vote

"Voting is the foundational benchmark for political action. Advancement is only achievable by seeking redress from local, state, and federal governments. To do this, the vote becomes essential." --- **Rev. Dr. MLK Jr.**

Throughout history, the power to administer elections and determine voter qualification has been regarded as lying in the State's control, not in the national government. All that the U.S. Constitution prescribes is that electors in each State must have the qualifications required for electors of the largest division of the state legislature. Because the qualifications for electors of the lower house of the state legislature are the state government's interest, it seems logical that Congress has no responsibility for deciding the qualifications of citizens entitled to vote within each State.

However, on several occasions, U.S. citizens have intervened to make declarations covering the right to vote. Today, many of the amendments of the U.S. Constitution ascribe to the right to vote. *The 15th Amendment proclaims that the right of the citizenry of America to vote is not to be denied or abridged by the U.S. or by any state on account of color, race, or previous condition of servitude.* That Amendment was essential because some southern states refused to allow blacks to vote even after the Civil War. The *19th Amendment* grants the right to vote to *women* and asserts that the citizenry will not be denied or abridged by the U.S. or any state on account of one's sex. Since the Civil War, various states, mainly in the South, have tried to prevent blacks from voting despite the provisions of the 15th Amendment. The establishment of all-white primary elections, the requirement of literacy tests, the imposition of poll taxes, and racial gerrymandering are discriminatory devices used to block black voters. The Supreme Court has since knocked them all down because they were made *unconstitutional* by the 15th Amendment and by the clause in the 14th Amendment prohibiting any state from denying to any person within its district *"equal protection of the laws."* Congress granted the federal government and the federal courts additional authority to make the voting rights in the 14th and 15th Amendments meaningful.

The *Supreme Court* has concluded surprisingly that literacy tests are allowed as qualifications for voting, even though federal statutes have outlawed them. Congress initially limited literacy tests and then amended the VRA to prohibit them entirely. The Court upheld these laws as a valid exercise of Congressional authority under *Section 5* of the 14th Amendment despite having the effect of overturning an earlier Court decision established in *Katzenbach v. Morgan* indicating that *Congress* may independently interpret the Constitution and even overrule the Supreme Court.

The *24th Amendment* prohibits poll taxes in elections for federal office. Specifically, it provides that the right of the citizenry of the U.S. to vote in any primary or other election for Vice President or President, for electors for Vice President or President, or Representative or Senator in Congress, shall not be denied or abridged by the U.S. or any state because of failure to pay a poll tax or other tax. The *26th Amendment* adopted in 1971 extends the right to vote to each citizen 18 or older.

Prisoners and Convicted Criminals Rights to Vote

"To no one will we refuse, sell, or delay, justice or right . . . no free human shall be imprisoned, or upon him nor send upon him, but by a lawful judgment of one's peers or by the statutes of the land."
- Magna Charta as quoted in *Griffin v. Illinois* (1956)

Some voting rights cases are concerned with the State's ability to restrict voting from persons convicted of a crime or imprisoned. States cannot withhold the right to vote to citizens awaiting trial and must provide them absentee ballots when there is no other viable option to voting. Once a person is convicted of a felony, the State can then disenfranchise the person permanently. When there is evidence of *racial bias* behind the law, a state is prevented from denying the right forever to vote to individuals convicted of a crime of corrupt nature. In several cases, the Court considered the duty of the government to provide absentee ballots to those awaiting trial while being incarcerated.

In *McDonald v. Board of Election Commissioners,* the Court dismissed a constitutional challenge to a state law that allows absentee ballots for individuals who are disabled or are outside the county the day of the election. The effect of the state law was to deny ballots to those incarcerated who were mainly indigent blacks and Latinos awaiting trial. However, the Court held in *O'Brien v. Skinner* that the State must provide absentee ballots to inmates who have no other way to vote. In O'Brien, the case demonstrated that the State refused to give inmates ballots and did not create polling venues at jails or even transport inmates to vote outside.

Inmates held outside their county of residence could receive a ballot, but those in jail within their primary county could not receive a ballot proving the state law was irrational. Thus, *McDonald* and *O'Brien* establish that the State cannot deny the right to vote to inmates awaiting trial. The State does not have to provide an absentee ballot if it permits alternative mechanisms for access to voting. If no such alternative exists, then a duty to provide inmates a ballot must be provided by the State.

Historical Significance of Suffrage in America

The longstanding history of the right to vote in America suggests gradual progress toward democracy. During colonial America, property qualifications restricted the right to vote, while voting rights today are open to all citizens by eighteen. Colonists viewed voting as a type of privilege while Americans consider it a fundamental right today. However, this perspective obscures eras where women, blacks, indigenous, and the impoverished were significantly disenfranchised. U.S. suffrage roots began in 15th century England. In 1430, Parliament blocked the vote in county parliament elections to landowners who produced a yearly profit of forty shillings and other criteria for their elections.

Laws excluded women, servants, aliens, and non-Anglicans. The *Charter of 1691* set up a condensed version of the *Election act of 1430*. In New York and New England, the forty shillings income was emulated based on size or value. Voters had to meet *racial, religious, and residency requirements.* Colonists disenfranchised dissenting *Catholics, Jews, Protestants, and eventually non-Protestants* until 1689. *Free blacks* were disenfranchised in every southern colony, and ten colonies also set up *residency requirements.*

Mostly half of the colonists' population remained disenfranchised, including men without property, slaves, women, freed black men, felons, apprentices, indentured laborers, and the mentally challenged. *Women* were obstructed because of a presumption of lack of sound reasoning. In Seneca Falls, New York, during 1848, almost three hundred male and female reformers proclaimed *women's right to vote. State laws and constitutions* always controlled voting rights. In 1865, after the Civil War, women hoped for national enfranchisement in conjunction with newly freed black men. Still, they lost as the traditional notion of a woman's place dominated among the distorted cognition of men in Congress.

The *14th Amendment* strategically promoted voting restrictions based on gender. Republican-controlled Congress enfranchised black men in 1870 when the *15th Amendment* blocked states from discrimination against possible voters due to race or existing servitude but not *gender.* The plan was to enfranchise black men to strengthen the Republican stronghold in the southern colonies. Blacks began to vote and use their political power to garner their other rights. White Democrats depended upon election laws and discriminatory apportionment to reduce the black and poor white political influence. By the 20th century, they imposed *poll taxes, property requirements, and literacy tests* to enact democratic hegemony. In 1916 the Republican and Democratic parties endorsed women's right to vote with Congressional approval in 1919. The *19th Amendment* was ratified, which granted *women the right to vote in 1920.* In 1971 the *26th Amendment* lowered the voting age to eighteen.

Conclusion of facts

"As an adjudicator of the law, with whole knowledge of historical jurisprudence, race must always be considered a variable."

Chief Justice Strickland (1986)

This book explores the historical significance, fundamental right of voting, and voting rights cases throughout our nation's origination. Research demonstrates the implicit discrimination towards vast segments of society from the right to vote especially impoverished blacks, indigenous, women, felons, laborers, the mentally challenged, and men without property or land. The history of racial caste in the U.S. would subside with the Civil War if the ideology of racial difference subsided when the institution of slavery was declared unconstitutional. Justice Harlan proclaimed that ***"Our Constitution is color-blind and neither knows nor tolerates classes among its citizens."*** However, the practices of a nation with a spiritual, moral deficit do not always conform to the Constitution's ideals, values, and principles.

The Framers of the Constitution were tasked with setting the spiritual direction of our nation. However, they failed to demonstrate biblical justice to all citizens, mainly enslaved impoverished blacks categorized as three-fifths of a person and chattel. To treat someone as less than human, one would have to dehumanize them, excluding their essential natural, human, civil, and fundamental rights. Laws are written to debase another man and promote slavery illustrates a lack of conscience, integrity, humanity, and the character of Christ. In choosing to discuss voting rights, I wanted to emphasize the hypocrisy of the post-civil war amendments "freeing the slave but ignoring the human" and the Court's flawed decision in dismantling preclearance requirements of the Voting Rights Act established in *Shelby County v. Holder*. The Fifteenth Amendment was ratified in 1870, granting black men the right to vote. However, black voters are still under siege by discrimination and racial bias of their fundamental voting rights today.

I speak for many when I say that racism white supremacy remains a cognitive disorder permeating the country after four hundred years and should be systematically dismantled. Man is flawed, deceitful, and broken. Judges err in their decisions based on selective originalism and textualism, and the Constitution has not lived up to its stated ideals. The letter of the law prevails; however, the spirit of the law remains unfulfilled. Only God is Supreme, righteous, and infallible, not man. Mosaic law is the highest law, and divine justice is the final word.

In examining voting rights from 15th century English origins to contemporary issues, one can see how far we have progressed in achieving first-class citizenship and fundamental rights for all citizens, how far we must continue, and what further responsibilities remain to be executed by the judicial, legislative, and executive levels of government, state and local governments and by the voting citizens of this nation. Implicit racial bias must be addressed and corrected in voting rights for every citizen regardless of color. Thus, the *Voting Rights Act* should be restored to its original condition with established preclearance as a remedy for voters of color and to mitigate undermining of representative government's legitimacy.

"This morning, we affirm that this fight must, and will, go on in the cause of our nation's quest for justice until every eligible citizen has the chance to exercise their right to vote, unencumbered by racial discrimination or unneeded procedures, rules, or practices."

Attorney General Eric Holder

"We cannot be disappointed by a Supreme Court decision that states we do not need such a necessary accouterment of the Voting Rights Act. A great democracy does not create obstacles to vote than to buy an assault weapon."

President William Jefferson Clinton

"50 years ago, I gave blood on that bridge in Selma, Alabama, for the right to vote. I will not just stand by and let the Supreme Court take a right to vote away from us. You must get out there and struggle and make America what it should be for all of us. We must state to Congress, 'Fix the Voting Rights Act!'"

Representative John Lewis, U.S. Congress

"The words are deceitful, dark, and ambiguous, such as no ordinary man of common sense would have used. They are selected to hide from Europe that in this enlightened nation, the practices of slavery has its advocates among leaders in the highest places."

Samuel Bryan, Abolitionist

"The Constitution bound the nation to do the bidding of the slave master, to bring out the full military power of the country, to dominate the slaves into obedience to their evil masters. The document is cunningly framed that none would have imagined that it sanctioned or recognized slavery."

Fredrick Douglass, Orator & Abolitionist

"You and we are different races, and your race suffers immensely, many of them, by living with us, while ours suffer from your presence."

President Abraham Lincoln

*"**Progress for the Negro has far too often been delayed and blocked**. Equality before the law has not always determined equal opportunity and treatment. The wasteful, harmful, and wrongful results of racial bias and segregation still appear in every area of life and every part of this nation. Discrimination hampers financial growth by preventing the highest development and utilization of our workforce. **It hampers our global leadership by contradicting at home the message we advocate globally.** The continuing attack on discrimination must be broad, private, pubic, and conducted at national, state, and local levels. **It must include executive and legislative action. Progression has occurred through executive action, persuasion, litigation, and initiative in achieving and protecting equality of opportunity in voting, education, employment, housing, government, transportation, and public accommodations.** However, pride in our achievements must not give way to an easement of our progress. Nor does progress in the executive branch enable the legislature to forego its responsibilities and duties."*

President John Fitzgerald Kennedy: Special Message to Congress on Civil Rights (1963)

"If my people who are called by my name shall humble themselves, pray and seek my face and turn from their evil ways, then I will hear from heaven and will heal their land." **2 Chronicles 7:14 NIV**

This verse is explicitly written to God's people Israel to bring needed revival to their nation. Racism is a spirit of evil, hate, division, and strife that must be destroyed. The race is a political and social construct that has no purpose in our inalienable, constitutional, civil, and fundamental rights. There exists a spiritual solution to every problem, and God does not require man's sinful deceit to achieve His sovereign purpose on earth. The sin has become this country's own, and so too, the need to cleanse. Advocating for voting rights and ensuring fair and equitable elections is God's work. Thus, as ambassadors of the gospel, we are bestowed as leaders to bring a resounding message of healing, biblical, and restorative justice as the salt of the earth. So be it. Selah. Ba'ruch haba beshem Elohim. Rosh Chodesh. Shalom. Every act of the law must be dealt with, and it is up to the African American law student to dig and uncover the problems in the law from its foundation. When the constitution was created, and the framers constructed the laws to be followed they did not consider the slaves and how it would be fair in the framing of the states and legal matters.

NOTE

What are your critical thoughts concerning these matters?

**Live life and trust in the one who called
you to knowledge King and Queens**

Knowledge is the key, and he is watching
your development belove

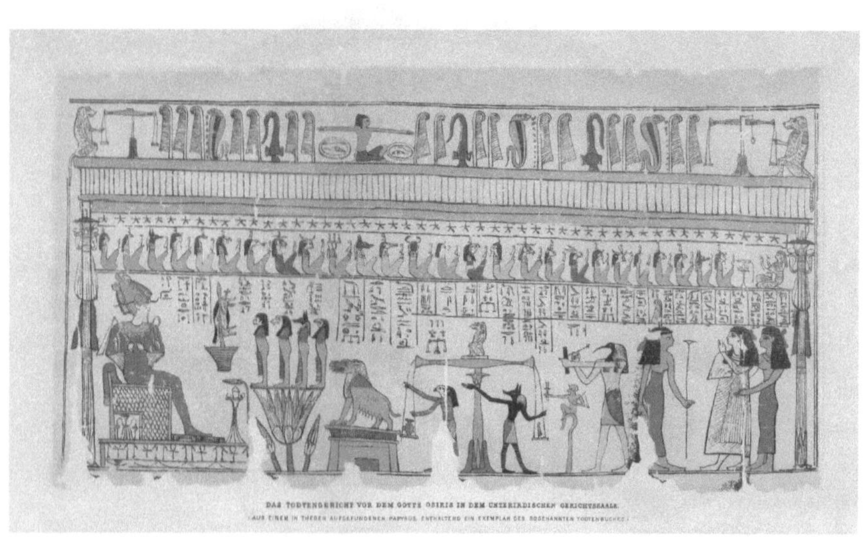

Hourus and Isis

Can we trust the words and the system?

REFERENCES

Alexander, M., 2011. *The New Jim Crow*. Mass Incarceration in the Age of Colorblindness. The New Press: N.Y.

Allen, D. (2021, March 01). A Forgotten Founder. The Atlantic. p 43.

American Political Science Association. *Style Manual for Political Science*. Rev. ed. Washington: APSA, 2001.

Baker, L. A., Gillette, C. P., & Schleicher, D., 2015. *Local Government Law. Cases and Materials*. 5th ed. West Academic: St. Paul, MN.

Brnovich, Attorney General of Arizona et al. v. Democratic National Committee, et al. Retrieved from www. supremecourt.gov/opinions/20pdf/19-1257_g204.pdf

Byrne, D. N., Ph.D. 2005. *The Editors of Black Issues in Higher Education*. The Unfinished Agenda of the Selma Montgomery Voting Rights March. Landmarks in Civil Rights History. John Wiley & Sons, Inc: Hoboken, NJ.

Cohen, A. (2013). *On Voting Rights, the Supremes' Most Notable Quotes*. The Atlantic. p14.

Chemerinsky, E., 2015. *Constitutional Law.* Principles and Policies. 5th ed Wolters Kluwer: NY.

Chiafalo et al. v. Washington, 591 U.S. 140 S. Ct. 2316 (2020). www.harvardlawreview.org

Crawford v. Marion County Election Board, 553, U.S. 181 (2008). https://www.law.cornell.edu

City University of New York. The Graduate Center. *Sociology Student Testifies Before Congress in Support of John Lewis Voting Rights Act.* Retrieved from www.gc.cuny.edu/News/ All-News/Detail?id=59931&gclid

DuVernay, Ava (Executive Producer). 2014. *Selma.* [Motion Picture Film]. Harpo Films; Cloud 8 Films.

DuVernay, Ava (Executive Producer). 2016. *13th.* [Documentary]. Kandoo Films.

Feinman, J. M., 2018. *Law 101. Everything you need to know about American Law.* 5th ed. Oxford University Press: New York.

Foner, E., & Garraty, J. A., 1991. *The Readers Companion to American History.* Houghton Mifflin Company: Boston, MA.

Franklin, J. H., 1980. *From Slavery to Freedom: A History of Negro Americans.* 5th ed. Alfred Knopf, Inc: New York.

Gans, D. (2021, July 7). Supreme Court Blog. Selective originalism and selective textualism: How the Roberts court decimated the Voting Rights Act. Message posted to www.scotusblog.com.

Garner, B. A., 2011. *Black's Law Dictionary.* 4th Pocket Ed. West: St. Paul, MN.

Hacker, D., 2009. A Pocket Style Manual. 5th ed. Bedford/St. Martins: Boston, MA.

Hannah-Jones, N., 2021. *The 1619 Project: A new origin story*. 1st ed. One World/Random House: N.Y.

Harper v. Virginia State Board of Elections, 383, U.S. at 663. https:/www.lexisnexis.com

Harvard Law Review et al. *The Bluebook: A Uniform System of Citation*. 18th ed. Cambridge: Harvard Law Review. Assn., 2005.

Kaplan, D.S., 2015. *An Introduction to the American Legal System, Government, and Constitution*. Wolters Kluwer: N.Y.

Katzenbach v. Morgan, 384 U.S. 641 (1966). https://www.law.jrank.org

Kramer v. Union Free School District, 395, U.S. at 626. Retrieved from www.lexisnexis.com

Nathaniel Calvin Lahey v. Commonwealth of Pennsylvania. https://m.imdb.com

Newkirk, V. R. (2021, March 01). *When America became a democracy*. The Atlantic, p 49.

New York Law School. Mendik Library. Retrieved from https://www.nyls.edu/library

Poor, H., 1984. *You and the Law*. The Readers Digest Association. 3rd ed. Pleasantville, New York.

Reynolds v. Sims, 377 U.S. at 555. https://www.supremecourt.gov

Rhimes, S. (Executive Producer). 2019. *How to get away with murder.* [Television broadcast]. Season 4 Episode 13.

Rothstein, R., 2017. *The Color of Law.* A Forgotten History of How Our Government Segregated America. Liveright Publishing: N.Y.

Shelby County v. Holder, 570 U.S. 529 (2013).

Speiser, S. M., 1993. *Lawyers and the American Dream.* M. Evans and Company: N.Y.

Sullivan, K., & Feldman, N. 2016. *Constitutional Law.* 19th ed. West Academic: St. Paul, MN.

Vance, J. W., 2020. Time. *Ruth Bader Ginsburg lost her battle to Save Voting Rights.* Retrieved from https://www.time.com/5890983/ruth-bader-ginsburg-voting-rights/

Westbury v. Sanders, 376, U.S. 1, 17 1964). https://www.roseinstitute.org

Yick Wo v. Hopkins, 118 U.S. 356, 370 (1886). https://www.supreme.justia.com